Poems of Mourning and Healing Memory

Poems of Mourning and Healing Memory

CARROLL E. ARKEMA

RESOURCE *Publications* · Eugene, Oregon

POEMS OF MOURNING AND HEALING MEMORY

Resource Publications
An Imprint of Wipf and Stock Publishers
199 W. 8th Ave., Suite 3
Eugene, OR 97401

www.wipfandstock.com

PAPERBACK ISBN: 978-1-5326-1963-2
HARDCOVER ISBN: 978-1-4982-9929-9
EBOOK ISBN: 978-1-4982-9928-2

Manufactured in the U.S.A.   JUNE 19, 2017

"Knees Shaking Uncontrollably" is reprinted from Springer Publishing's *Journal of Religion and Health*, vol. 56, 2017, pp. 74–76, "Knees Shaking Uncontrollably," by Carroll E. Arkema, DOI 10.1007/s10943–015-0097–3, with kind permission by Springer Science+Business Media New York.

Dedicated to

Oney Arkema
(1897–1974)
Paternal Grandfather,
Farmer, Construction worker;

and

Arnold Sadwin
(1927–2015)
Psychiatrist—
each of them a Healer

Contents

CONTENTS

Preface

IN THE COURSE OF putting this book together, it dawned on me that I was picking up where my previous book *Beyond Me* had left off. The final poem in that book, entitled "Hands," was a tribute to my parents, and ended with an account of my last visit to my mother and her death ten days later on August 24, 2013.

My Dad lived almost two years after that, alone in the house they'd shared for forty-five years. He got along fairly well—continuing his wood-working in his basement Wood Shop; attending Church; and looking forward to almost weekly outings with my brother Ken, occasional visits from my brother Dean and his wife Gayle, and infrequent visits by Mairead and me. Ken and Pat lived an hour away in Iowa City; Dean and Gayle in Denver; and Mairead and I in New York City and New Jersey.

In early May, 2015, Dad had a heart attack. He was hospitalized for a few days, and was then admitted to a Nursing Home, where he lived for about six weeks. He initially hated being there and wanted to go home, but he gradually settled in and made a few friends in the dining hall. Church friends and family members visited him almost daily, and then early in the morning of June 14 of that same year (2015) he had another heart attack and died instantly.

The first half of this book consists of poems of mourning—beginning with my poetic Eulogy for my mother, followed by poems about my Dad's grief over her loss, continuing with my transfigurational last visit with him, my Eulogy for him, several poems of mourning and remembrance, and concluding with the aftermath of the auctioning off of all his tools and their earthly possessions.

The second half of the book contains poetic memories of my parents, other relatives, a friend, an influential Psychiatrist, a former patient in my psychotherapy practice, and other memorable experiences. The poem "Engaging Aging" is my response to a Rembrandt self-portrait which stunned me with a recognition of my own aging and mortality.

Prose poems are a format with which I was unfamiliar when I began writing several years ago; in case you haven't come across them either, I want to mention that three poems are in the format of prose poems: "My Eulogy for my Dad," "Knees Shaking Uncontrollably," and "Charcoal Headstone Tracing."

I wrote all the poems in this book over the course of three years. Many are about healing, and writing them has been healing for me—a major way of coming to terms with the death of my parents and of remembering and honoring significant people and experiences in my life. I hope that reading them will trigger your own memories; resonate with various layers of your experiences; help you move through your own grief; and perhaps encourage you to do some writing of your own!

Acknowledgments

I'VE BEEN ENCOURAGED AND supported by so many people over the three years of writing these poems, especially again from Roger Plantikow, Mairead Stack, my brother Ken, Dan Bottorff, Charles Mayer, Don Ferrell, Michele Galante, and Sal Barone. My brother Dean, his wife Gayle, and Ken's wife Pat have also affirmed my writing, excitedly welcomed my first book, and look forward to this one.

All these people have helped me believe in the value of my writing when I've had times of doubt, and I'm extremely grateful!

I've also felt believed-in, encouraged, and affirmed by the many Endorsers of this volume, whose names you'll see on the back cover and inside the front of the book.

What happens in writing is a mysterious and awesome thing, and I'm profoundly grateful to the "Muse," or the "Spirit"—whatever name one gives to that Force or Energy which prompts me to write and keeps me at it until a given poem is completed. I love the entire process, while at the same time wondering—after I've read a poem I wrote a few weeks or months or years earlier—who wrote that? Did I write that? Insofar as the Spirit wrote through me, it wasn't all me.

It's as if the poems have a life of their own, and speak to me from their autonomy. I'm moved, sometimes awed, and mostly grateful. Grateful for everyone and everything that's involved in my writing, including my Mom, my Dad, Grandpa Oney Arkema, and the others you'll read about.

I didn't start writing poetry till I was sixty years of age, and I feel so blessed and grateful to have discovered this gift.

One final acknowledgement: you wouldn't be reading this if not for the Editors, Publishers, and Artists at Wipf and Stock Publishers who've believed in me twice now. They've guided me through the process, and have been supportive partners in publishing this book.

When all is said and done, I'm grateful for life, Life; love, Love; and creativity, Creator.

GRAVEDIGGERS' SOD

"Over there's the sod, Son;
that's where they put it
until this is all over with."

He's standing in front
of the open grave
the day before
the funeral and
interment of his wife.

His voice
is just above
a tense whisper,
the words squeezed
through clenched teeth,
throat rasping in an
altered state of speaking.

"The thought of her
being there in the ground:
phew! Pretty hard to take, Son.
Hard to take! Man oh man!"
in that same raspy voice,
shaking his head.

Hearing him, my gut aches.
I'm a bit more removed;
he's ahead of me here.
She's my Mom, and
I know she's dead,

that she'll be buried
here tomorrow,
but I'm not there yet.

Which means he's even more
alone, without her, without
me really being there.
But I say, "Yes, I see,
that's how they do it."

I'm getting there.
Maybe that's
enough for now.

PORTRAIT OF MOM: MY EULOGY

For her last five years she suffered
from congestive heart failure;
and the last two years of her life
she dozed and slept a lot—
even at Dad's Craft Sale
that final year of her life.
She insisted on being there.
All three sons were there,
and she wouldn't be anywhere else:
"Being there is interesting," she said,
when invited to stay home.

Osteoporosis bent her half-double
but couldn't cripple
her determined pleasure
to help put those
deep blue tablecloths
on the display tables
as she always had.

The day after that craft sale
she got shingles on her back!
"They hurt so bad," she said.
It was the last thing she needed:
the chronic pain
draining even the last
bits of energy. "I just wish
I'd get my pep back,"
she often said.

For years she had knitted afghans
in unforgettably striking,
varied, and colorful patterns.
Now she had no more energy,
which was sad to see.

Spiritually, however,
she was read to die—
had been for a couple
of years already.

Her life light was dying out,
but the life she lived
still shines brightly.

Of hardy Iowa farm-girl origins,
she was the oldest daughter of ten—
surrogate mom for several siblings,
enduring resentment from them.

Her own mother was sweet, devoted,
gave all she could—probably too much—
to raising children and gardening;
died of lung cancer too young,
at sixty-one. Mom's father—
a hard-edged Dutchman,
rigid, skin of steel,
inaccessible emotionally,
derisive, laughed off pain
or distress, his own
as well as that of others—
soldiered on through
pain as they all did.
But I'd catch my Mom
and her mother crying
quietly in the kitchen.

Through her adult years
my Mom would rise, arise—
her grit like dough
powered and kneaded
by spiritual yeast—
to stand up to her Dad
and increasingly also
to my Dad!
It was heartening for me
to see that Feminine power—
which those men so feared—
glow, grow, create, endure!

Her faith was an inner fire,
a flame burning, never quenched.
Ladies Society at Church
and Golden Hour, which
she attended religiously,
fed that flame,
nurtured a life of
quietly serving others and
nurtured the love she gave—
selflessly, with smiles,
knowing every name,
every heart.

Generous, but no fool,
she had a look when talking
about people who were phony:
a turn of the head,
a feinted "pooh!"

A woman of her patriarchal era
and beyond, she shone brightly.
Bridling a bit, she accepted her lot,
her era, but it didn't define her heart.
She was way more than that:

she glowed translucently
with divine light.

When greeting anyone,
she'd approach with a quick step,
up-bend a bit, raise her head—
hair always coiffed—and say,
"I'm so glad to see you folks,"
and smile with genuine charm.

Being with people was
something she loved.
Dressed to the nines,
she loved compliments,
but blew them off, saying,
"Oh, thank you, but
I've had this outfit for years."

Her constant love,
the way she carried herself
in a forward-leaning but
well-grounded energy,
moving to connect, to relate,
will always inspire me.
The way she carried her
vulnerability with dignity
and at times a sigh
is a mystery to me.

But that's just it:
She brought me to mystery,
the Mystery which
to me is God.
She connected me
to that Mystery
by the way she lived
more than by what she said.

As part of her faith,
she must have had her doubts:
if God is love, why such suffering,
heartache, pain? How can people
be so cruel and mean?
But she unerringly believed
that God suffered with us—
as shown especially in Jesus;
and I believe that she rarely
conceived of herself as other
than alive in Him,
and living for Him.

More than I've known
until writing this poem,
she's an ongoing inspiration,
connected to that same source
of Love and amazing Healing
that flows through me
when I'm in tune.

It's hard for me now that she's gone,
not living there in that Sully home,
being there whenever I'd return
with my partner or alone—
eager to see me,
always believing in me.

Back then she was in Sully,
waiting to see me, greet me;
now she awaits me, will greet me
in that ultimate spiritual home
whence she's gone.

NEEDS COMFORT

With his huge,
Peasant-farmer,
Eighty-seven year old
Arthritic hands

He carefully
Reaches out
To gently touch—
Actually lightly pat—

The rectangular
White box
With a clear
Plastic top

Through which
Lusciously glow
Six alternately
Black and white

Iced turnovers
Apple-filled.
"There you are,"
He seems to say.

He buried
His wife, my mother,
Yesterday. But is
Now less alone:

The turnovers
Are there.
Life goes on.
Needs comfort.

EIGHTY-EIGHT, NOW ALONE

He falls asleep in his chair.
Startles awake
Talking to her:
She isn't there.

It's months since she died.
His life goes on.
When he's awake she's gone,
When he's asleep she's home.

GOODBYE TO DAD

We flew to Iowa
To say goodbye
To my dying Dad;

Spent the weekend
Visiting him
In the nursing home

Named St. Francis Manor—
A Roman Catholic affiliation
Normally anathema to him.

He was in pain.
It was agonizing
To witness him

Restlessly writhing—
Abdomen rolling, chest
Heaving in every position

As he shifted from
One direction on the bed
To the other end.

Gasping, grasping eyes
Looking for relief,
Finding none:

Probably saw his pain
Reflected in my eyes
Back to him.

Much restless dozing,
Then awakening accusing
"Them" of making him

Eat something which
Didn't agree with him,
Regretting he'd eaten.

Laboring to make sense
Of his pain, longing
To be in control again,

Fighting the
Creeping grip
Of diminishment.

Heart at twenty percent,
Kidneys at twenty-five;
How long could he live?

Everyone uncertain.
A few months yet?
But organs failing.

Sometimes he'd sit up
As always, socialize,
Ask questions, reminisce;

Able to sustain
That condition only
Briefly before tiring.

Admission yesterday
After hospitalization,
He's still settling in.

Eighty-nine, formerly
Strong, now unsteady,
Speech slightly slurred.

Shocking transition
For him and us:
Never going home again.

Gut-wrenching:
Him physically,
Him and us emotionally.

Mairead and I are here
For a long weekend—
Three days visiting.

Most likely we'd never
See him alive again:
This goodbye not routine.

But Monday morning,
When the time came,
The time came

To go, I told him
"We're leaving, Dad."
He was able to stand.

"Got to go?" he said;
"Well, glad you came."
"We are too," I replied.

I shook his hand.
Mairead was waiting,
Looking at me questioningly.

I didn't understand; I
Nodded to her as if to say,
"Time to say goodbye,"

Which she then did;
She hugged him, crying,
Said, "Goodbye, Dad."

"Wait," he said, "I'll
Walk you to the door."
He did, as always, but

Unsteadily, not the same.
What to say, O what to say?
There we left him standing.

We walked away
Down the long hall,
Me crying, Mairead sobbing

So violently she
Was stumbling. I put
My arm around her.

From the depths of herself,
Gasping, she said, "Why . . .
Didn't you hug . . . your Dad?"

"He wouldn't want that,"
I said. But I had punted,
Projected, began to get it.

In the lobby now,
Both sobbing, we met
My brother Dean.

I was holding Mairead,
Dropped my cap;
Dean said, "I'll get it."

A nurse guided us
To a conference room,
Me of course wondering

Why didn't I hug my Dad?
This would most likely
Be my last chance ever.

Throwing down my coat
And cap, I burst out
"I'm going back!"

I did; almost ran
Back down that hall,
Entered his room.

He was sitting
On the side of his bed,
Looking forlorn.

I walked over,
Stood in front
Of him, crying,

Said, "Dad,
"I've never hugged you,
But I want to."

He stood right up,
We hugged; neither
Saying anything,

Standing there facing
Each other; I said,
"We're a spiritual family."

True to form, he said,
"Yes, one of the best."
"Due largely to you," I said.

"Mom [my mother] always
Said," he added, "Jesus
Will not be ashamed

To call us brothers
And sisters."[1] "I know,"
I said, really crying now.

I sensed that by now
He knew this could be
Our last time together.

Sure enough, he gave
It words, "If we don't
See each other again,

We'll see each other
In the after-life then."
"Yes, yes," I said, and left.

I think I saw him
Sit back down on
The side of his bed.

Stumbling down that hall,
I was sobbing more
Than I think I ever have.

Something transporting
Had happened, which I
Recounted to Dean and Mairead.

"Ah, so he knows then,"
Dean said, "that
This may be the end."

I nodded, still recovering
From what had been
An overpowering experience

---

1. The Holy Bible (NRSV), Hebrews 2:11b.

On a spiritual plane.
We said goodbye to Dean,
Drove to the airplane.

It took me days to return
To day-to-day living
From something that profound.

I understood the scripture
That was spoken through him
To me from my Mom

At a deeper level
At the time than I can
Easily articulate now:

Something about how
In the Spirit world,
Relationships are redefined.

It was an experience
In those few moments
Of empowering peer-ship

Which he was creating
By quoting Mom's love of
That verse from Scripture—

That even Jesus is not
Ashamed to call us
Sisters and brothers.

Several days later
A further insight
Made my heart

Leap for joy like
Elizabeth's baby when she
Learned of Mary's pregnancy.[2]

I felt stir inside me
The centrality of
Femininity in the

Divine economy.
Did you notice it
In this visit to Dad?

It was the question
Birthed in pain from
The depths of Mairead

That presented me with
The opportunity to
Change my ways—

To break free of the
Anti-emotional charade
Of tough masculinity.

Then it further rocked me
That my Dad had uncannily
Drawn on femininity

When he quoted to me
My Mom's/his late wife's—
A woman's—favorite verse!

It was remarkable for me
To suddenly see
A perfect congruity

2. Ibid., Luke 1:39–45.

Between these two
Transformative events—
Both mediated by women!

The central importance
Of the feminine role
Was doubly reinforced

By the fact that
My Dad didn't have to
Mention his wife at all,

And he normally wouldn't have,
And by the fact that he
Said "brothers and sisters"—

A gender-inclusive
Translation, unlike
The one he's always used.

It's always exhilarated me
That many scriptural stories
Work counter-culturally.

To turn upside-down
What we normally see so that
We can see a new reality,

Which reorders human
Priorities to favor
Equality and vulnerability.

I knew something new
Had been offered me, that
Something was at work in me;

And when I took
The opportunity
To break free

Of the guarded ways
I'd learned to be,
I was rewarded doubly:

By my Dad also
Relating differently,
Embracing femininity!

It's like we were all
Living out live a scripted
Spiritual story;

And the Spirit's transformative
Healing energy
Continues its work in me!

Now, of course, the waiting;
But in many ways
The most important things

Have already happened:
Those deepest connections,
Which are everlasting,

And which—due to Divine
Love and forgiveness—
Are not broken by death.

The loving, the Loving.

MY EULOGY FOR MY DAD

This will take a few minutes, because I want to celebrate the Holy Spirit in the life of Bernard Arkema. Bernard would be really uncomfortable with me for focusing on him as a person, but I'll honor him as Bernard, a man of God. He might have let me get away with that. His connection to the Spirit made him a better man than he could have been without it—which is true for all of us, of course.

Bernard Arkema was a powerful man,
> physically, spiritually, and artistically.
> He had high standards, was good at so many different things,
and had those same high standards for me.

I knew he had an amazing inner relationship with God, and that that relationship was reinforced by his close relationship with his father Oney, whom he called "Pa." They prayed together, and those prayers grounded his faith in God, so that when Oney died, Bernard was sustained by faith and prayer. Bernard lived by a Latin phrase that Oney loved: *ora et labora*: "pray and work."

Bernard had high standards spiritually, too, for himself and for others. He spoke his mind about what he understood as right and wrong. But underneath his strict faith, he had a loving heart.
> Which came out most tenderly with his grandchildren and great-grandchildren,
> and also in his placing love over judgment when it came down to a choice.

I witnessed that non-judgmental love after I met and married my ex-wife at Princeton Seminary. I worried about whether he'd accept as a daughter-in-law a female minister—which she became. But then I was amazed at how he related to her. He'd ask her about her ministry, and he understood the joys and trials of clergy because of being an Elder in his Church and working with clergy here in Sully. He totally accepted her as a woman minister.

By his own admission, he could be stubborn and find it difficult to apologize—to my mother also, but over time it became clear to me that that was just a defense against his vulnerability and emotionality. He loved and depended on her. When they were hit by a speeding car while crossing the street here in Sully, and my mother's neck was broken, I was away on vacation from the church in New Jersey where I was a Pastor. But he called me about what happened, and he was in tears. Amazingly, she fully recovered from her broken neck!

We didn't see a lot of that vulnerable side of my Dad, but it was there. I saw it also once between him and Oney; and in his total dependency upon the Holy Spirit; and certainly in his friendship with his brother-in-law Junior Rozendaal, and others of you.

He loved to sing hymns.
  He lived to pray.
  He loved to work.
  He loved the art of woodworking.
  He made a five-piece miniature wooden train set just 6 months ago for the 3-year-old great-grandchild of one of my best friends.

One of the most impressive things about Bernard is that he made a major change in his life in the direction of doing more of what he loved: he was an excellent and respected farmer, but at the age of 40, he made the decision to move to Sully to work at the Lumber Yard. He'd always loved woodworking, and this nine-to-five job gave him more time to perfect and refine his art. He was an equally excellent Lumber Yard Foreman. As Foreman at the Sully Co-op, he shaped and trained many men to be more competent and more ethical, which enabled them to feel better about themselves and their work.

But throughout his life—on the farm and at the Co-op—it was his art that oriented and restored him. When Mairead and I would come to Sully for a visit, we'd be sitting in the living room of my parents' house with Dad and my brothers and sisters-in-law, and after a while Dad would say, "Well," sort of to himself—he'd awaken from silence or a doze and say, "Well . . . " quite often. Then he'd get up and leave the room; I'd assume he was going to the bathroom. We'd all keep talking, and about half an hour later we'd suddenly wonder, "Where's Dad?" Sure enough, he'd be in his Woodshop in the basement.

Ora et labora: pray and work.

Woodworking was a form of prayer for him, which I'm sure is true for all of you when you're doing what you love to do.

God is in the love of each other,
and in our love of what we do.

Bernard is gone. Bernard's gone home.

He was such a powerful presence; it's hard to believe he's gone.

As close as he was with God, we know—as the apostle Paul wrote—that he was only seeing through a glass darkly; now he sees face to face. What a glory, what a joy! None of us really know what the afterlife is like; it's beyond our imagining. But in some way, Bernard is now with Cornelia, with Oney, with Junior Rozendaal, and all those many saints we heard about when he read the Bible after every meal. Abraham, Moses, Elijah, David, Peter, Paul—all those flawed heroes of faith whom God loves; and Rachel, Deborah the Judge, Ruth, Naomi, Mary the mother of Jesus, Elizabeth, Anna the prophetess, Lydia, Dorcas. He may initially have a little difficulty accepting the female saints as equals, but they'll straighten him out.

On the other hand, some of his last words to me were to remind me that Cornelia, my Mom, used to love to say that "Jesus will not be ashamed to call us brothers and sisters." It was the Spirit at work transforming him that led him to say "and sisters."

In 1968, Bernard moved an entire house from a farm to the town of Sully, remodeled it, and he and Cornelia lived there until they died. All the while, God was remodeling Bernard, and now God's moved Bernard to God's home.

SOUTHERN COMFORT

"A shot of Southern Comfort,
Right here," he had said,
Face wincing with
A sucking-in breath,
Pointing with his left hand
To his heart,
Clearly in pain.

We had laughed,
Surprised,
Thinking he was
Kidding or
Hallucinating—
Having never
Known him to drink
Anything like that.

He looked annoyed,
Said, "No, seriously,
It helps," wincing again.

This was the day after
His admission to
The nursing home,
Five days after
He was hospitalized
With a heart attack.

We told the story
To my brothers,
We all chuckled,
Thinking he must
Have been addled,
Mentally confused.

Five weeks later,
After he had died
Of a second heart attack,
We were all gathered
In his house;

I looked in his refrigerator
For something to eat,
And what did I see:
Sure enough, a bottle
Of Southern Comfort!

We all looked
At each other
Incredulously,
Mouths agape.
"He was serious
That day," I said;
"He must have
Been medicating
Himself for his
Heart pangs
With Southern Comfort
For quite some time."

I felt stricken
By all he'd lost,
And by his helplessness
Near the end.

He was wrenched away
Against his will—
Of necessity, yes,
Being no longer able to
Take care of himself,
But taken nonetheless—
From his ways,
From his home,
From all he'd known.

He'd also been
Wrenched away
From his remedy
For his heart pain—
Pain which he may
Or may not
Have known
Presaged
His death.

With pain I recall
That look
On his face,
That gesture of
His, pointing
To his heart.

Could one say
That the final
Remedy for him,
From that gasping,
Grasping pain,
Was death?

A STRANGE THING

Here's a strange thing:
I somehow saw my Dad
More clearly
After he died,

More fully imaged him.
Perhaps because he
Was no longer
Physically there,

I had to actually
And actively use
My imagination
To recreate him.

I began to remember
How he walked
How he sat
How he talked.

This was triggered by—
For the first time—
Focusing on the mole
Next to his nose

As he lay dead
In his coffin.
I had seen—yet
Never really seen—

That mole next to
The lower right
Side of his nose
A million times.

It grabbed me that day;
My throat tightened.
Strange to notice it when
Seeing it for the last time.

It made me wonder
What else I hadn't
Ever truly seen
About him.

After he died
He became less
My Dad somehow,
More an equal.

The authority,
Elevation, hierarchy
Of the "Dad" position gone—
A loss and a gain.

I'm remembering
How he walked
Those last five years
Before he died at eighty-nine:

Shoulders slightly stooped,
Arms hanging straight
Down, not swinging
By his sides as he moved.

More and more he shuffled.
I often feared he'd stumble

And fall face-forward;
Could he catch himself?

In his wedding photo
He's standing proudly
Straight and tall,
Six-foot-two.

When he'd sit down lately,
He'd sort of back up
To his recliner, then,
Let himself drop.

Probably his elderly legs
Were no longer limber
Enough to bend and hold
Him as he sat down.

When sitting down to table,
He could be more graceful,
Using his arms to help
Ease himself onto a chair.

He'd more often talk
As if emerging from
A considered reverie,
Offering his conclusion

Or asking a question;
Seemingly disengaged
But then rallying;
Usually opinionated,

But more frequently
In those later years
A bit more tentative,
Less need to prove

His certainty,
More willing to let
Some doubt and
Listening emerge.

This was poignant to see,
Because I feared
He'd have so little
Time left to be loved.

He lived bravely
His whole life,
The fourth of twelve,
Competing for love

As a child, then finding
A woman he loved
Who loved him more
Than he could himself.

Grateful to God for her,
But waging a lifetime war
Against his vulnerability,
Thus limiting intimacy.

She died two years
Before he did, leaving
Him more lost and lonely
Than he could fully admit.

Probably a useful thing.
He maintained his
Usual routines: dozing;
Woodworking; worshipping

At the same church
In the same Iowa town

He was born and raised in.
His faith sustained him.

He did start talking
More about his feelings
After she died
Than he ever had,

Which was a blessing—
Him being more open.
It made connecting
With him a bit easier;

Which makes his absence
Harder to bear;
But he was aware
Of the transience

Of all life forms,
Including his body:
The inherent entropy
Countered by creativity—

As captured by the prophet Isaiah:
"The grass withers, the flower fades;
But the [creating] word of our God
Will stand forever."[1]

For me now, Dad is present and gone,
Gone to his eternal home.
But the Spirit which inhabited
Him for his time lives on.

1. The Holy Bible (NRSV), Isaiah 40:8.

HIS APRON

His green carpenter's apron
Hangs from the bench vise
On the left front side
Of his woodshop workbench.

It's splotched with so many
Spots of different colored paints
That it reminds me of
A Jackson Pollock painting.

My breath catches in my throat
At the thought that my Dad
Will never wear that apron again.
He died at the age of eighty-nine.

I feel a further pang of pain
Just below my heart as I see
The four wooden carcasses of green
John Deere tractors he started.

They sit there on his workbench
Next to the apron, unfinished—
Witnesses to the ongoing systematic
But individual handiwork of his Art.

Starkly the carcasses pose
The question "Which wins:
Death's definitive end to life
Or creative Spirit which never dies?"

But could it be that both are true:
It's not a matter of win or lose.
The unique man Bernard is gone
AND his witness to Spirit lives on.

It's a fact he'll never work again,
Never finish those nascent tractors.
He'll never wear that apron again,
But Spirit, toys, memory live on.

SUNRISE SURPRISE

Located and blinded
By a brilliant crimson sunrise
Which seems to have refracted
All its bursting rays
Dead center into
My rear view mirror,
I quickly flip the mirror
To its night-vision setting
To see where I'm going.

"Damn, look at that sunrise,"
I say to my brother Ken
As we're heading west
Down Interstate eighty
From Ken's home to Sully, Iowa,
In Dad's old two-thousand-two
Buick Le Sabre. Ken turns, looks,
Says, "Man, every time
We open our eyes, there's
A new painting by God!"

We're en route to the estate sale
Of what remains
Of all our parents' earthly possessions.
Dad died three months earlier,
Mother two years before that.

Their house and what it's stuffed with
Is all that's left, and everything

Will be auctioned off:
Colorful afghans she knitted,
Walnut furniture he crafted and
She sanded, finished, polished;
Woodworking tools from his Shop;
Walnut wood he'd hunted down
In local farmers' creeks and fields,
Then cured in a solar drying shed
He'd designed and built himself.

All must go, we hope—be sold—
Including the very car we're riding in,
And eventually the house.

People are gathering today
In that one location—
Like those sun rays
This morning converging
In the rearview mirror.

It's a final sunset
Of our parents' lives,
But we're surprised
By a sunrise we can't ignore
Penetrating our soberness
With the light of a new day.

PIANO TRANSPORT

On a sunny Sunday morning in September,
watching birds from the screened-in porch
of my brother and his wife's Iowa home,
I was roused from my post-breakfast reverie
by a sudden burst of notes from a piano
filling the air with the music of old hymns.

Drawn to the source of this sound from inside,
I walked quietly into the living room
and was transfixed by what I felt and observed:
my sister-in-law Pat at the piano
with her back to me and totally absorbed
in playing those hymns I had known as a child.

I lay down unheard on the sofa behind her,
sinking into the cushions and letting myself
be transported to a world beyond the mundane
while she played a medley of those old hymns
which—along with many treasured Bible stories—
are woven into the very fabric of my being:

Amazing grace; For the beauty of the earth;
This is my Father's world; The Lord's my shepherd;
O God our help in ages past; Praise ye the Lord;
Come Thou fount of every blessing; Breath on Me
breath of God; O Master let me walk with Thee;
Take my life and let it be; Abide with me.

Too soon she stopped playing.
I had just lain down it seemed;

but yes, we had to get moving
if we were to get to church on time.

My very joints seemed to be disjointed:
my body seemed to be and to not be mine.
I knitted myself together and stood up,
Came back to this world from the sublime.

Off we went to the Sunday Worship Service
where nothing there compared to where I'd been:
lying there transported on the sofa
listening to Pat playing those ancient hymns—
perfect timing, because we had just the day before
auctioned off all our parents' earthly possessions.

That Saturday too had been a beautiful day:
the last time we'd gather at the family home
now that our mother had died two years prior
and our father just three months ago gone.
The Spirit expressed in those hymns had midwifed me
in my biological birth and then in coming alive within.

Pat's heart beating into the pounding of that piano
throbbed with a love of Spirit that transported me,
reminded me of the Love which pulses through this
world and the universe—Love which I easily forget
and am reminded of in love, in nature, in beauty,
in creativity, and even in endings and death.

"For the beauty of the earth,
for the beauty of the skies;
for the love which from our birth,
over and around us lies;
Lord of all, to thee we raise
this our hymn of grateful praise."[1]

1. Folliott, S. Pierpoint. (1864) Used by permission of the author's estate and of Oxford University Press in The Hymnbook. Richmond, Philadelphia, New York: John Ribble, MCMLV.

DAD'S PILLOW

With wide-eyed wonder
at about age eight,
standing in the next room,
I caught my Dad
half-gently
punching his pillow
with his powerful
arm and fist
into perfect shape
until it was just right
as he lay down to nap.

He lay his head on it
twice to test it,
then relaxed into it
with a blissful look
and soon thereafter
fell asleep.

At now sixty-eight
I know just that feeling:
me, my pillow,
and blissful sleep.

Seeing him do that
planted a seed
of empowerment
that grew in me:

that I could shape

something simple
as a pillow
to suit me
rather than
accommodate
myself to it.

KNEES SHAKING UNCONTROLLABLY

On a predawn summer morning in our modest house on the farm, I awoke to a strange new sound, riveting me with alarm even before my twelve-year-old mind could put together what it was. Already quaking, I thought "Can that be my Dad crying?" Not just crying, but sobbing! I had never in my life seen, heard, or known him to cry. I had to install a new category.

By now fully awake, I heard him say—in bursts of speech accompanying his sobs—"I gotta go see Pa, I gotta go see Pa," in a voice which he was trying to hush. I could hear he was in a rush.

He was talking to my Mom in their bedroom around the corner from mine. Not a sound from her.

I remember lying perfectly still, frozen; thought of myself as hiding. I knew he wouldn't want to see me. Clearly this was an emergency about something going on in him. I heard him getting dressed, then going out the door of the house. He didn't slam the doors, probably wanting to think we were asleep. I heard him open the door of his "fifty-one" Chevy pick-up truck that he drove whenever he was going anywhere by himself. I heard the old thing start up, then quietly leave the yard. I can't find words for how I felt.

For many minutes I couldn't move; still no sound from my mother, my two brothers still asleep. Then suddenly I just had to move, couldn't lie there passively, though I had no idea what to do. Stealthily I got up, got dressed, went out into the family room and lay on my back on the couch. There was a sour taste in my throat, which I had to swallow so as not to choke. But the thing I remember the most to this day is that my knees were shaking beyond control. That had never happened before. My body was registering and quivering with terror before my mind could get there.

I thought of the cows: before long they would need to be milked; but I didn't know how to do that. Next thing I remember is that I was in the barn. Something in me took over; the structural

rhythms I guess of life on the farm—previously background—
were now foreground, with me playing a new role beyond what I
felt prepared for. But somebody had to fill the role of getting the
cows into the barn so their udders could be drained of milk every
morning and evening.

As I was following the last cow into the barn to stanchion them,
I heard the familiar crunch of gravel: Dad's pickup rolling onto
the yard. I saw him go into the house; my heart thumping in my
chest. He emerged and came towards the barn. I hardly dared look
at him, but he took thought for me and said, "Everything's gonna
be all right. I talked to Grandpa; we prayed, and he said he went
through the same thing when he was my age." Hearing this, I was
astonished, even as I began to feel relief. My stomach relaxed back
into place, the compressed air in my chest left, and things did be-
come all right again.

He proceeded to milk the cows, and I carried the milk to the milk-
house. I've been digesting this event ever since. It's probably the
reason that I've become a Psychotherapist. I was awed that talking
to someone could have such a dramatic result—specifically when
that someone had been where you'd gone. "The same thing had
happened to him": those words kept reverberating in my brain. An
immeasurable thing a father can give a son: No, you are not alone.

My Dad never confided in me the content of his desperation; but
the remedy itself highlights the clues imbedded in the events. My
uncontrollable shaking reveals a frightening crack in the cohesive
functioning of my being. The threat to relational order and daily
function loosed existential terror and ultimate doubts about the
cohesiveness of the universe: in the face of which my mother froze,
I shook, and my Dad fled for help.

My Dad's experience seems to me a personal version of what
Yeats gave voice to after World War I: "Things fall apart; the cen-
ter cannot hold;/ Mere anarchy is loosed upon the world."[1] Yeats
concludes the poem wondering if hope is again being born in
Bethlehem.

Nicodemus, a leader of the Jews, came to Jesus by night (as my
Dad to my Grandpa), troubled, because he had perceived and
acknowledged that Jesus was "a teacher who came from God; for
no one can do these signs that you do apart from the presence of

1. Yeats, William Butler (1920). "The Second Coming," Michael Robartes and the
Dancer. Churchtown, Dundrum, Ireland: The Chuala Press.

God." "How can these things be," he wonders.[2] Jesus talks about rebirth: indicating that that's how fundamental this level of disorientation is: one needs to get reoriented, reborn spiritually in order to be part of divine order.

The fact that prayer was a central ingredient of the healing of my Dad, along with what my grandfather said, suggests that my grandfather had experienced the same existential terror and had survived by a connection to Spirit—which was deeply stabilizing.

Many years later I learned that my Dad—the fourth of twelve children—had felt emotionally shut out and rejected by his mother. This left him with a deep underlying insecurity and doubts about his worth, and makes more understandable his seeking out his father—whom I also learned later was emotionally estranged from his wife, but had found his core identity, peace, and purpose in his relationship with Spirit.

I loved this Grandpa, I knew he loved me: he related to me, talked respectfully, was interested in what I might have to say. He had strong opinions, especially about his faith. But he was accessible. He just loved people. I noticed him delighting in each and every grandchild, not just me. I felt no envy: I felt accurately seen, which was all I needed: being seen lovingly; positively believed in for my potentiality, for who I was and could be.

I also knew that for him, God was a living reality, anchoring his identity; which helped me believe the miracle that morning that brought my Dad inner peace.

I too have known that nighttime terror. I awoke in my mid-thirties feeling abandoned, alone, comfortless—discovering that I couldn't be comforted by a human embrace. Feeling without resources, I too resorted to prayer. My own therapist had helped me see my need to nurture my connection to Spirit. Prayerfully breathing deeply, my hyperventilation eased, and I slowly felt peace, along with the hope of resuming my daily routine.

What gives deepest peace? What's the meaning of this journey? Is life meaningful or empty? We all have doubts, anxiety, insecurity. Amidst this, our deepest security is connection to Divinity. In my Dad's dark night of the soul, Grandpa mediated Divinity incarnationally—in the flesh—communicating that he knew the same insecurity, but that life is a spiritual journey, which includes

2. *The Holy Bible (NRSV)*, John 3:1–10.

insecurity; but deeper than that, while we work and pray, we can find our core identity in a loving Divinity.

That connection to Spirit set my Dad free to resume his daily routines—a changed person inside, a little less dependent on another human being. And the memory of that incarnation—Grandpa mediating God in flesh—lives on after Grandpa's death: in my Dad, certainly, and also, as you can hear, healingly in me.

CHILDHOOD PASTOR

I was thirteen when an unfamiliar car
drove hesitantly onto our farmyard that summer,
pulled carefully alongside our car, and parked.
I just happened to be nearby that afternoon
and watched with amazement and some
embarrassment as the car door opened
and the minister of our church got out.

He peered around as if he was in a foreign country
and didn't know which way to go—a bit lost.
He was tall, thin, with wire-rimmed glasses
on a narrow face topped with blond hair;
he had on a long-sleeved white shirt and tie;
wore dressy shoes a bit scuffed: was overall
dressed in a way farmers dress only for church.

I couldn't imagine what he was doing here:
no family member had died, nor was seriously ill,
nor had done anything scandalous I was aware of.
He nodded to me and I gave a faint smile
but didn't move; I sensed he was looking
for an adult. Finally, he said, "Is your Dad home?"
I said "Yes, I'll go see if I can find him," and ran.

I heard the "M" Farmall tractor engine roaring
behind the machine shed, and went to get Dad.
When my Dad and I returned, he was talking
to my Mom, who'd come out of the house to greet him.
"What's he doing here, Dad?" I half-whispered.

"I'm not sure," my Dad said, half-ignoring me.
"Greetings, Pastor, surprised to see you here."

Becoming gradually more at ease,
Reverend Van Someren said he'd come
because he wants to visit every member
of the congregation at work or at home
in order to get to know them better.
I was amazed, had never heard of such a thing,
but began to feel something I didn't understand.

My parents invited him in for coffeetime.
My two brothers and I were there too,
but I don't remember what they talked about.
Half an hour or so later we all got up
and except for my mother we all went outside.
I assumed he was leaving, and that my Dad
and I would go back to our work and chores.

But no, he wanted to see more, be with us longer,
get to know what we do. I began to feel moved.
Love! The feeling I couldn't quite name before.
Loved. He walked with us to the barn, didn't seem
to worry about getting manure on his shoes.
That touched me as deeply as Jesus washing
the feet of his disciples.[1] He walked in our shoes!

He asked questions; he didn't preach, nor lecture,
he wanted to be taught: to learn what's involved in
farming: feeding pigs, grinding grain, milking cows.
I felt that—to him—who we were and what we did
was as important as who he was and what he did.
He even climbed up on a tractor seat. When he left,
he didn't need to say a prayer: God was there.

---

1. The Holy Bible (NRSV), John 13:1–20.

PORTRAIT OF AUNT LIZZIE

My Great-Aunt Lizzie—
Born without a hip socket
On her pelvis' right side
In the eighteen-nineties
In the Netherlands—

Immigrated to the U.S.
At age thirteen with
Her parents and three younger
Siblings—my grandfather,
Oney, the youngest, aged three.

She was almost sixty
When I was born—
In her sixties when I
Got to know her
When visiting her home.

She lived alone
On the churchyard
In this one-story
Whitewashed
Tiny house originally
Built for the church sexton.

Because of her handicap,
She never married,
Nor, in that era—
And being religious—
Ever slept with a man.

My parents and my two
Younger brothers and I
Would visit her
About every two months
For coffee, juice, and cookies.

I was both afraid of her
And fascinated by her.
She was short of stature
And walked with a cane
And a sort of hefting limp.

By that time in her life,
The top of her right thigh bone
Had been surgically grafted
Directly to her hip bone,
Leaving that thigh unable to bend.

So she lifted, twisted,
And turned forward
As she walked, with the
Assistance of a strange cane
To help her keep her balance.

She sat on a tall stool
At the slightly elevated
Rectangular table
In her small kitchen
Where she served her goodies.

She always served
Dutch windmill cookies,
Which had a somewhat
Sharp, cinnamon-ginger
Flavor we kids loved.

We had to wait a few minutes
After knocking on her door
For her to come hobbling
From her back sitting room
To open up and let us in.

Through her window
Beside the front door,
We kids could see her coming,
And hear her cane
Thumping on the floor.

Always glad for company,
She rarely went outdoors,
Which was also a mystery
To us kids, and of course
Seemed a bit weird.

My mother was more at ease
With her than my Dad,
So they had an arrangement
That my Mom and we kids
Visited her while my Dad

Went to a Men's Society
Meeting next door at Church,
After which he'd stop in
Briefly to be with us
Before we all went home.

We kids were also fascinated
By the fact that her house
Was wired such that she could hear
What was happening in church,
Especially Sunday morning Worship.

She couldn't truly sit down,
Because her hip didn't bend.
The wooden chair she sat in
In her sitting-room-den
Where she sat with visitors

Had a semicircular cut-out
On the right front side
So that she could sit
With that thigh aligned
Straight with her upper body,

Thus allowing her lower leg
And foot to reach and rest
On the floor. It worked for her.
She spent most of her time there,
Reading, knitting, embroidering.

She could stretch out
Straight in bed to sleep.
We kids never dared ask
How she went to the bathroom,
But somehow she managed.

Two things about Aunt Lizzie
Moved me most: still move me:
Her love of my cousin Milo;
And the thrill she got
Listening to all-male singing.

Milo was a couple years
Younger than me: sensitive,
Intelligent, often smiling,
Different in those specific ways
From all of his brothers:

Middle child of five sons,
Apple of Aunt Lizzie's eye.
And she wasn't really shy
About people knowing it.
I did feel a bit of envy.

Why was he her favorite?
Because Milo, bless his heart,
Was always physically short,
Not exactly a dwarf in height,
But obviously different.

He was self-conscious about it.
But Aunt Lizzie, God bless her,
Identified with his being different.
He loved and needed that; they
Lit up when with each other.

The other poignant memory
I have about Aunt Lizzie
Is how she'd get when
She knew men-only would
Be singing hymns in church.

My Dad would occasionally
Confide in me about her—
His father's oldest sister—
"You know, Son, she has desires
Just like every other woman."

He'd shake his head,
Say no more, expel his breath;
He almost could have wept.
"Her siblings all married,
She was never with a man."

He'd also bemoan to me
The pain she'd suffered
As a child and young woman
Before the doctors fused
Her thigh to her pelvis:

"Can you imagine, Son, the pain?
With every move she made,
The end of that bone
Moved around in there
Unanchored, poking flesh.

She'd sometimes scream,
But she never gave in;
She worked, got jobs doing
Housework, taking care
Of other people's children.

What a blessing back then
When Grandpa John got word
That they could fuse that bone.
She was in her thirties then.
What a blessed relief that's been.

But all those men singing, Son,
You know now what I mean?"
It did make sense of what I'd seen
When we'd be visiting her
During a Men's Society meeting.

She'd have that speaker
Turned on, volume low,
While we were visiting
During those meetings—
One ear listening.

She had come to know
Pretty accurately
When it would come time
At the end of their meeting
For those men to sing hymns.

At that point she'd move
Remarkably fast
To turn up the volume.
Her face would light up
And she'd be transported.

She didn't need to die
To go to heaven;
She was there then.
It was glorious:
Her with those men.

Her physical abnormality
Closed some doors,
But opened a door she entered
To a Reality not easily seen
Undergirding this one.

With an echo of her childhood
First language, Dutch,
She'd often say,"Innahow,"
As she finished talking
About a particular subject,

So now I say, "Anyhow,
She lives on in me,
In my memory,
And in what
This poem can only
Barely convey
That she revealed to me:
God in Lizzie's body."

HEARING

I was astounded to learn
That the clothes
I was wearing
Were audible—
Made noises, sounds.

I could hear
The fabric of my shirt
Rustling as I moved.

I asked my Mom
If she'd ever heard
Clothes rustling.

She was riding in
The passenger seat
Of my parents' car
That I was driving home
In Iowa at sixteen
After having seen the Eye,
Ear, Nose, and Throat doctor
To have my ears cleaned.

She chuckled
A little doubtfully,
But listened.
She caught my mood,
Said she didn't think she had
Heard such a thing;

But I could tell by her tone
That she was not dismissive—
Was willing to believe me.

Something about the way
She was with me that day—
Taking me seriously,
Learning from me—
Made me feel like a man.

I'd gotten my ears cleaned,
Was taught by the doctor
How to clean them properly,
Heard my clothes rustle;
But it was the way
My Mom listened to me—
Enjoyed me that day—
That led me to write this poem.

I'd gotten my ears cleaned,
But it was my Mom
Who heard me.

LIFE LETTERS

Mother was
With father
Before I
Was born,

Continued through
Thick and thin
Before and after
I left home.

Loved me, fed me,
Let me go;
Was as scared as I
As I moved on,

Wrote letters
In reply
To my
Letters home.

For forty-nine
Years this
Exchange
Went on.

Immersed
In immediacy
My life
Moved on.

Occasionally
I visited home,
But the writing
Went on.

Once when visiting
Her at eighty-four,
She brought out
A large box.

She was
Giving me back
All my
Letters and cards.
I wasn't
Surprised
That she had
Kept all of them;

But I didn't
Understand
What she was
Doing that day.

I mailed
That box
To my
Home address,

Stored it
Under my bed,
Mostly forgot
About it.

For the next
Couple of years,
She tried
To write back

To me and
My brothers.
But she was
Getting mixed up.

Congestive
Heart Failure
Was taking
Its toll.

The last year
Of her life,
She sent no
Letters at all.

Two years
After she died,
My partner
Took out that box,

Began reading
My letters,
Was amazed,
Touched, shocked.

She urged me
To read them;
I read,
I cried.

There in those
Letters to Mom
Was the history
Of my life!

Now I'll never
Know for sure

If my Mom knew
What she was doing.

But as I read
My own letters,
Written to her
Through the years,

I'm receiving
Again, from her,
My life
In loving detail.

Through flesh
And through words,
Love gives birth
And rebirth.

THAT PATH PAST THE HOUSE

I'm haunted by that narrow path
between my parents' garage
on this side and the neighbor's
property on that side which was
bounded by a lattice fence
overgrown by vines and flowers.

My Dad walked it often
to and from the back yard
to get un-planed walnut planks
from his woodshed out back
which he would then carry
to his basement woodshop.

Long before the new neighbor
put up the boundary fence,
school children would walk
morning and afternoon
as a shortcut to get to
and from the bus stop
on the next street over
behind my parents' house.

My parents would watch them,
get to know them by name,
knew the families they came from,
gave them cookies and blessings
after school as they walked home.
For thirty-some years this went on,

generations of children growing from
kindergarten through eighth grade.

When occasionally I'd visit home,
I'd notice that around the time
for the schoolkids to be going by,
my Dad would get a bit restless:
his attention would drift to them,
their passage a part of his routine.

We their children were long gone,
lived far away from them
and didn't get home often,
so their grandkids rarely came.
These neighborhood kids filled in.

DID ONEY SEE ANGELS?

We were standing outside
near the picnic table—
my Dad and I—on a bright
crisp autumn day at my
house near New Paltz, New York,
during my parents' annual
weekend visit from Iowa.
My mother and my partner Mairead
were in the house preparing lunch.

My Dad's normal way of being alternated
between a meditative quietness
and an escalating intensity of talking
which at times led
to a depth of discussion
having a biblical religious focus
but could devolve into a desperate
assertion of what he believed or
a querulous disbelief that others
could believe differently than him.

One could, in either case, be impressed
with his focus on the ultimate
meaning of life and how to live,
but then one usually began to feel
brow-beaten rather than invited
into a respectful discussion
of different points of view
which could have been mutually enriching.

On this visit, he was probably
seventy-five and I fifty-five.
I had left home at seventeen
to go to college, yes, but also
to get some room to breathe—
away from the oppressive atmosphere;
and over the years, I had learned
how—during visits—to be with him
in ways least intolerable.

I learned to steer the conversation
in a constructive direction
by asking about our family history,
especially about his Dad, named Oney,
whom I knew he was close to
and loved.

By the time of this visit,
Oney had been dead twenty-five years.
I had known Oney, too,
until I was twenty-five;
had worked alongside him
on a construction crew
when he was supposedly retired
and I was in high school.

I had enjoyed working with him,
in part, yes, because I felt
seen, known, respected,
and loved by him.
But I also just enjoyed
Being around him.
He enjoyed me,
was himself around me,
and I was myself around him.

He saw the potential in me,
and I knew the depths in him
because I'd spent hours
on Sunday evenings in his home
listening to him tell stories,
discuss the Pastor's sermon,
preside over the conversation
with four or five other men—
his sons or sons-in-law—
and me once I'd reached thirteen.

He knew how to laugh—
he and I used to laugh too
while working construction—
at our foibles, stupid mistakes,
and those of other men,
and at the unexpected
surprises in life which
turned our heads on end.

His maturity and spiritual stance
had come at a physical price—
as he told it, not only AT a price,
but BECAUSE of this price—
of losing his arm below the elbow
in a construction accident,
due in part to his frustration
with a machine and carelessness.

He'd felt shame, wounded pride,
no longer invulnerable,
briefly suicidally angry at himself.
What had been routine prayers
before the accident
now began to mean something:
he felt God within and all around,
and gradually got used to
his prosthetic arm.

No longer physically whole,
he was now a whole new man.
This is how I had come
to know my Grandpa;
but my Dad of course
had known him for my Dad's
whole lifetime—called him "Pa."

As important as Oney was to me,
he was even more so to my Dad.
My Dad was the fourth of twelve
children, and for some reason
his mother emotionally rejected him;

which left my Dad
with a deep feeling
of insecurity and self-doubt,
which I eventually
understood led to
a kind of desperate desire
for people to pay attention
to him, agree with him,
and support his beliefs.

I always felt his pain
beneath the pressure,
though I didn't understand
the dynamics of it till later.
My Dad's faith and spirituality—
modeled and reinforced by Oney's—
kept him sane and
ameliorated his pain.

Remarkably intelligent,
competent and creative,
with exacting standards,
he became a successful farmer,

then improved on Oney's skill
in woodworking and
became a master craftsman,

built grandfather clocks
and all kinds of furniture
in his basement Shop
out of Iowa walnut that
he himself solar-dried.

Always haunted by that
core abandonment wound,
he was not at all times
crippled by it.
With the help of his faith,
he could transcend it.

Back to my Dad and me
at the upstate picnic table:
I said, "You know, Dad,
I have a memory of Grandpa
once saying he'd seen angels.
Do you think that was true?

I had his full attention!
He paused, looked at me
as if to assess whether to tell me—
whether I believed enough
to merit such information—
tried to talk, choked, teared up,

said, "Oh yes, Son, he saw them;
he was in a field somewhere,
heard some wind, looked up,
and saw them fly past;
they were brown, he said,
then they were gone."

I felt so close to my Dad then.
As I said, Oney was dead,
but his spirit and the Spirit
which had inhabited him
lived on in my Dad.

So did Oney see angels?
My literal mind has doubts,
but I believe he did.
Maybe that's the point:
I don't have to see
in order to believe.

Whatever Oney saw
was beyond him
but a revelation:
a glimpse of reality
that humans don't easily see.

There was something about Oney—
the way he lived, the way he loved,
what he could see—that at his best
made Oney himself a revelation,
a manifestation,
of the kind of human
that I believe Holy Spirit
wants us to be: angelic.

We could each see
and be an angel
if we were open to it.

My Dad didn't often get teary,
but recalling this story
moved him deeply,
and I sensed divine energy,
binding us all three spiritually:
Oney, my Dad, and me.

HIDDEN TREASURE

They found a hundred-dollar bill
in her underwear drawer
while removing her clothes
after she had died;
another between the washcloths
in the bathroom linen closet,
a few more she'd stashed
in the beautiful walnut
fold-out sewing cabinet.

They found more "hunnies"—
as my brother called them—
two years later
after our Dad had died
and we were preparing
to auction off
all their possessions.

Our parents had moved
from the farm
into that house
in small-town Iowa
and lived there
for forty-five years
after we three sons
had left home.

She'd been a housewife
and mother on the farm.
What to do now in town?

Well, she had always been
tidying and cleaning their house,
so within a couple of years
she'd found at least two
weekly cleaning jobs in
the houses of wives who
no longer wanted to do that.

The pleasure she got
from doing this
was difficult for me to imagine
until I realized that, for her,
she was now getting paid
for something she'd
been doing all her life anyway!

Modest and self-effacing,
in addition to never having
earned her own money,
she talked of how she
enjoyed the cleaning—
never mentioning the money.

But here it was!

She did spend some
on jewelry for herself—
mostly costume, only
a couple expensive pieces.
Dad built her an intricate
four-foot-high polished
walnut jewelry cabinet
with doors and many
red-velvet-lined drawers
and compartments
including necklace hooks.

It took weeks before
we sons finally found
a ring set with an
expensive ruby stone
that the daughters-in-law
had seen her wearing.
It was in Dad's gun closet!

Little mysteries
and idiosyncrasies
posthumously
consistent with
a personality
that guarded and hid
some of its treasures.

SIDE MIRRORS

"Nah, not giving up
my car keys,"
Dad said in a calm
matter-of-fact voice.

His tone revealed
that he, eighty-eight,
expected respect
or there might be
hell to pay.

The side mirrors
on his two-thousand-two
red Buick Le Sabre
were a sight
to behold.

The outer shell
of each mirror
was still intact,
but the mirror
parts themselves
were frozen
inside the housing
with a bright
green cement,

at an angle
at which they
allowed the driver

to see behind
the car adequately—
although the mirrors
were now unable
to be adjusted
from the inside
as originally.

Aside from a
small dent on
the passenger-side
front fender,
he had no further
major accidents

nor minor scrapes
till he died
six weeks after
he was admitted
to the nursing home.

Seven years earlier
he'd totaled his
beloved Chevy S10
pickup truck by
making a left turn
directly into the path
of a large SUV.

Hospitalized
three weeks then
with a hematoma
on the brain
which they drilled
into his skull
to drain,

he recovered,
passed his
neurological and
renewal driver's
license tests, and
safely drove
that old Buick
until he died
at eighty-nine.

CHILDHOOD BEST FRIEND

I had a best friend
from second grade on,
who first drew me out
of my haze
of fear and isolation.

He sat down next to me one day
on the school bus going home.

By then I had already withdrawn
into an inner world
to try to shut down expressing myself
in any way which would arouse
my father's disapproval
and corporal punishment.

I realized even then, at age seven,
that I had created a facial mask—
consisting of my own skin and features—
of smiling compliance,

which I became aware of
because at times I'd be smiling
in response to a teacher or peer
when I was being called upon
or teased,
and my smile would break,
my mask would crack,
and I'd inwardly panic,
for fear of being discovered.

The disparity between
inner and outer
was so great
that at times
I couldn't fake it.
My stomach ached,
I felt scared,
seen through,
and trapped.

Thank God I was smart,
did well in school, and
was well-behaved
for the most part:
I tested the rules
in school a bit,
but soon learned
that any misbehavior
would be reported
to my Dad at home;

therefore in school too
I was careful
to behave
so as to prevent
any punishment
or rebuke
from my Dad
when I got home.

It was while living
in that fog of fear
and vigilance
that Bob bothered me
for several days
until I let him in.

I was surprised, puzzled,
even irritated at first,
tried to put him off;
I turned away,
tried to ignore his silly jokes.
I felt bothered,
intruded upon;
safe inside,
wanting to
be left alone.

But thank God again,
Bob would not be put off.
So much so that I complained
about him to my Mom,
who must have told my Dad,
whereupon—irony of ironies—
it was my Dad,
whom I had originally
walled myself off from,
who one day casually said to me,
"You know, that boy on the bus
who's bothering you,
I think maybe
he wants to be your friend.
It's good to have a friend."

That incongruity
was very confusing
to a child of that age;
but that intervention
by my otherwise scary Dad
changed my life.

It took many years
before I could begin to accept
that a parent who inflicted

so much pain on me,
and of whom I was
constantly afraid,
could have a good side;
that all people
(except me of course)
have both a good
and a bad side.

In any case,
over the course
of that year in second grade,
Bob and I became
inseparable friends.
Our friendship lasted
all the way through college,
and began to end
when I went east
to Princeton Seminary
and Bob remained
in Iowa.

I still remember saying goodbye
at the end of that last summer.

We'd both spent that last summer—
after we'd graduated from college—
back home, living in our
respective homes,
and working weekdays
at our respective jobs.

Several evenings each week
after a day's work,
and especially on weekends,
we'd hang out at Pizza hut
or in some bar,

talking about all
kinds of stuff—
from girls to parents to
religion and politics—
in often impassioned ways
the way one can
with a heart-to-heart friend.

We knew I'd be leaving
at the end of that summer
for Princeton,
and that that
would mark a major change
in our relationship—
something of the magnitude
of an end.
But we never talked
about it much,
I think because
for both of us,
it would have been
too hard to bear.

A few years earlier,
perhaps after eighth grade,
he actually cried one night
as we were standing
outside his house
near my car
as I was getting
ready to go home.

He was telling me
for the first time,
with a venomous but
helpless tone,
that his father fairly regularly

beat his mother.
Bob loved his mother, and
was therefore heartbroken
and enraged; hated his dad,
but didn't know what to do.
His older brother
and two older sisters
had done nothing to stop it;
so he didn't know what to do.

I don't know what I said,
if anything.
I'd never heard of,
nor even imagined
such a thing.
But that night
cemented our friendship.

His father apparently
never hit the children,
only his wife.
He would periodically
receive shock treatments
for depression
in some hospital in Des Moines.

It was our mutual sharing
about the domestic violence
in each of our lives
that contributed to our bond.
Even children, I'm convinced,
sense unconsciously
each other's wounds,
which was probably one factor
that led Bob to connect
with me in the first place.
Thank God we had each other

to share our pain with—
spoken and unspoken,
a deep resonance.
Our respective burdens
were definitely made lighter
from sharing them.

I was anxious but also excited
about my huge decision
to go east to Princeton—
so much so, I realized later,
that I failed to notice
Bob's unspoken sadness
over being left behind.

I don't think we even hugged
as we said goodbye;
we Iowa guys didn't do
that sort of thing.

But at some deep inner level
which I was avoiding
by focusing on Princeton,
my heart was a bit broken.
It was a necessary, inevitable,
but nonetheless painful
thing to part that night.
I know he wished me well,
and me him, and I know
that in fact our friendship
was a major factor
in giving me the courage,
ironically, to leave him.

We rarely communicated
when I was in Princeton,
wrote letters occasionally,

though seven months later
he was the Best Man
at my wedding.

After that, we drifted apart,
gradually lost touch.
It seems like that's
how it goes with friends.
But my life would be
totally different, I know,
without Bob having
broken into my life
back then.

THE PSYCHIATRIST

He moved like lightning from room to room;
I had to walk fast to keep up with him.
It had echoes of when I was a little kid
trying to keep up with my Dad on the farm.

Arnold Sadwin was visiting his patients
in the hospital's psychiatric ward; and
as part of my CPE Training program,[1]
he had invited me to accompany him.

I've never forgotten what happened:
it was like being in a whirlwind.
I was frightened and in awe of him;
I had no idea how much I would learn.

He would swirl into a patient's room,
greet them by name, shake their hand
if he sensed that it wouldn't frighten them—
then be like the still point in a hurricane.

He carried a pen and pad in hand,
sat down usually facing the patient—
sitting fairly close, which heightened
the electric charge between them.

---

1. Clinical Pastoral Education (CPE) is a supervised training program for Chaplains in a Medical Center, Psychiatric Hospital, or other ministerial setting for those who want to become a Hospital Chaplain or an Imam, Rabbi, Priest, or Pastor. This program had five Student Chaplains and two Supervising Chaplains. Arnold Sadwin, M.D.(1927–2015), was a Psychiatrist who consulted with us for an hour each week about any patients we wanted to understand better, which of course also helped us to get to know ourselves better.

Each patient knew that something important
was about to happen; they trusted him:
maybe even got sick so they could see him—
knowing he'd zero in on the core of their problem.

Indeed he did. It's only after forty years—
thirty-five of them as an ordained Pastor
and Psychotherapist myself—
that I can better understand what happened.

With some patients, he didn't even ask
how they were doing before they began.
They knew that the time would go fast,
so they too zeroed in on their problem.

"You're a failure, a goddamn failure!"
one patient yelled at Doctor Sadwin.
"Ahh, it's hard to live with your father
cutting you down like that all the time."

When Sadwin said that, I was stunned!
To me, it seemed clear that the patient
had just brutally attacked Sadwin!
How then could his response be so calm?

Back then I was only a beginner.
I had had only minimal experience
dealing with internalized demons,
let alone the unconscious and transference.

I was taken aback and astonished
that Sadwin didn't take this personally
nor question his own competency—
though he did add, "I'm always learning."

He wasn't undone by the patient.
In fact, I think that's what was healing:

that he didn't let the patient or the
patient's brutal internalized father

set the terms of the present relationship;
instead, he entered the patient's inner drama—
letting the patient be the father this time,
while himself taking the part of the patient,

but in this exchange not being undone,
because he was also Arnold the healer,
who voluntarily stepped into the drama
yet remained himself also outside of it.

He thus connected deeply with
the patient as the recipient of these
attacks, while also modeling
not letting the father set the terms.

It's like Arnold's meta communication
to the patient's internalized father
was, "Bring it on, you bastard,
you're not gonna do us in;

you and your son here are in need
of healing; I'm his friend, and yours,
but your abuse is keeping you from feeling
your own pain by inflicting it on your son."

The patient was indeed in tears
when we left—feeling, no doubt,
his own as well as his father's pain.
All this took place in three minutes.

I could feel the healing that day,
but had no concepts to understand it—
especially since that patient wasn't likely
to leave the hospital and live a changed life.

The conscious mind wants something
more dramatic—thereby misses the profound
healing that happened because Arnold shared—
and thus helped that patient bear—his suffering.

Immediately upon entering the next room,
the male patient began to whine
with the voice of a frightened five-year-old,
"I tried, I tried, I tried to be good!"

I felt the anguish and fear in my gut,
had no idea what I would have said,
might not have been able to speak;
but thank God Sadwin the healer was there.

"Ahh, mother's still disappointed in you,"
he said, as he sat while the man wailed.
No further words of encouragement—
except to say in a soft voice with a handshake,

"I'll be back in a couple of days."
Any other words, I see now, would
probably have been heard by the man as
yet another criticism of where he was.

Once again the meta message was
"I'm letting you and your mother know
that I'm here with both of you right now,
and I'll be back without disapproval."

We visited five or six more patients,
each time with Arnold zeroing in
on the core wound and reframing
the inner drama on healing terms.

I see now that he had gotten to know
each patient's central crippling relationship

and stood with the patient in it without
being destroyed, and outside it with love.

He radiated and communicated
care and respect for the wounded core
of the patient as well as for where
the patient was at any given time

and for whatever amount of openness
the patient had for contact and healing.
He neither stormed nor scorned
the patient's defenses—even psychotic ones.

I experienced and observed with Sadwin
what I later learned cognitively:
that a person's psychotic defenses
are helping them—are the best that

the person can do to keep it together,
to keep them from acting out
murderous rage towards themselves
or others, or from being a weeping puddle.

One respects the defenses and realizes
that the more primitive the defenses,
the more severe the wound—whether
from childhood or any kind of trauma.

It is invaluable for a chaplain,
therapist, or any helping professional
to know these concepts: they help
the Healer understand what's going on.

The concepts actually fortify the Healer
to endure assaults and bear the sometimes
overwhelming suffering which
the Healer experiences with the patient.

But is there any point to these
three-minute intense encounters
if the patient still needs the hospital
and may in fact never fully leave?

What is healing, really? Living or
behaving in certain ways defined
as acceptable or normal by the
majority or the people with power?

Or spiritual presence;
deep loving connection
with any human no matter
what the situation?

I experienced with Arnold that day
that we were not visiting psychotic
patients but individual persons
who needed psychotic defenses.

It began to change my life,
face me in a new direction,
give me a new understanding
of what we read of Jesus' ministry.[2]

When Jesus entered the territory where
"a man . . . with an unclean spirit"
had been hiding in the tombs
and could neither contain himself

nor be restrained with chains,
the man ran out to meet Jesus and
bowed down before him for help.
Jesus spoke directly to the demon

---

2. The Holy Bible (NRSV), Mark 5:1–20.

in the man, saying, "Come out of the man,
you unclean spirit!" Through the man's mouth,
the demon said in a mocking voice,
"What have you to do with me, Jesus,

Son of the Most High God, do not
torment me." The unclean spirit,
who was tormenting the man,
accused Jesus of being the Tormentor!

Jesus stood strong, did not take it
personally, but addressed the demon
relationally, and upped the ante
by asking, "What is your name?"

The spirit raises him one,
and says, "My name is Legion,
for we are many." But they're
beginning to show vulnerability:

the demons beg Jesus not to send them
out of the country. With our current
understanding—analogous to respecting
defenses—Jesus respects even the demons,

whom, we can imagine, were the ongoing
powerful energies of the man's parents,
internalized and tormenting him with
what we now call "voices," or "bad objects."

The story portrays the real-life power
of those dark negative energies
by telling how Jesus grants their plea
to leave the man and enter the pigs.

The pigs don't have the psychic resources
to contain or manage the dark energies,

which then enter them and cause them
to rush to their death by drowning.

The local economy is impacted
by the healing: relationships are altered
and people are more frightened by
the effects of healing upon the economy

than by the torments of the possessed man,
who ends up changed and "in his right mind."
A closer reading of the story highlights the fact
that Jesus—as Sadwin did, too—was relating

to the wounded man, yes, but also to the demons.
In fact, it's not clear if they're really separate:
the demon uses the singular and plural pronoun:
"My name is Legion; for we are many."

Again, with our current understanding,
we think in terms of a fragmented self,
which leads us to wonder if it's the man—
not the unclean spirit—who begs Jesus

not to send the spirits out of the country.
These spirits had been part of the man's world,
part of his "self," so he didn't want them
banished: he needed to get to know them.

He needed to name his demons, as we also
need to know and name our internalized
destructive parental figures. The man also
understandably cared about the demons.

He may even have thought he needed them,
but Jesus knew that he needed to see how
destructive these spirits were, so he let
them enter the pigs and be exposed as deadly.

The man then thought he needed to remain
with Jesus, but Jesus frees him, gives him
an independent purpose as a healed man:
to talk about the Spirit's healing power.

Again, is it essential to know all of this
if we are therapists or healers?
No, the Spirit has been healing people
for centuries with, or in spite of, us.

But the concepts—casting out demons,
Externalizing bad objects—help us know
what's going on, which strengthens us
when we're in a vulnerable place.

As the patient releases internal demons
or bad objects in a trusting relationship
with the therapist, the patient observes
the therapist withstanding the venom or hate

and not retaliating. And by externalizing
the feelings, the patient gains some distance
on the intensity, and increasingly separates
his or her core self from the destructive

internal objects—or, as it was described
in Jesus' day, from being possessed by demons.
How important it is, then—and hopeful
to keep telling the story, the old new story.

I needed Dr. Sadwin that day in order
to learn that Healing is a caring
relationship in which I name my demons
while realizing that they're not me:

I need no longer live on their terms;
I can work at being someone new

whose life and identity bears witness
to the love and mercy shown me.

Jesus said, "Go home to your friends,
. . . tell them how much the Lord has done
for you, . . . what mercy he has shown you."
The man did, "and everyone was amazed."[3]

3. Ibid.

EYE CONTACT

On a warmish winter day,
walking up the street,
I lifted my eyes and
saw her coming towards me,
being pushed in a wheelchair.

She was slightly slumped,
half-sitting, half-lying,
a bit twisted in the seat,
seeming to be relaxed or resigned,
as if she'd been there a long time:

a Down syndrome woman,
elderly, perhaps even sixty.
Of all the people on that street
God knows why
I looked into her eyes.

Her eyes locked
onto mine, returned
my gaze; I saw eternity
in hers, perhaps she in mine;
I kept moving, was past,

all so fast that I'm still
dwelling in that past
unpacking what I saw:
A plea from her—
"Can I have more?"—

was there in that gaze,
which lasted mere seconds
but opened upon eternity,
profoundly shook me.
What had I seen in her?

My own dependency
longing for connection
with fellow humanity,
which paradoxically
is equally scary, such that we

scarcely stop to dwell
there, to look deeply
into another's eyes, to see
each other's finite infinity,
and our primal need to be seen.

It reminded me of a Bergman film
in which at the end a young man
longing for a connection
with a remote father says after
it happens, "Papa spoke to me!"[1]

Or of Jesus, interrupting his
walk and talk when the
desperately bleeding woman
touched his garment unseen,
turned, saw her, and said "You're whole!"[2]

1. Ingmar Bergman, Through a Glass Darkly.
2. The Holy Bible, Matthew 9:22.

ALL THERE IN THE EYES

With this patient[1]
More than any other,
It's all in the eyes.
All the healing
That's going on
Is captured
And conveyed in
The eye contact
Between us as
She enters the room.

I walk down the hallway
To the waiting room
To greet her;
We exchange a "Hi,"
A nod, or a smile,
And she follows me
Down the hall
To my office.

I step just inside,
Holding the door open
And stepping aside
So she can pass.
I turn to face her
As she comes through.
I wouldn't have to

---

1. Identifying information has been changed to protect the identity of this former patient.

Look up into her eyes
There, but I do, and
She looks into my eyes too.

It's become a ritual,
Part of what we do,
Every session, every week.
One couldn't say
It's so important
That almost nothing
Else need happen,
But that's almost true.
It's hard to say in words
All that's exchanged there.

The simple beauty
Of her eyes is
Breathlessly arresting;
There's a bit of daring,
Strength, and confidence,
While also an
Infinite softness,
Looking for love,
Respectful acceptance,
Notice of who she is.

She sought therapy
For anxiety attacks.

The first panic came
After her third
Child was born—
The previous two
Having been twin girls
Three years earlier.
She felt overwhelmed,
No longer free,
Unable to get away.

As we explored
The roots of these
Anxiety feelings,
She remembered she'd
Felt trapped at home
As a five-year-old:
Had packed a bag then,
Told her parents she
Was running away.

They laughed at her,
Offered to take her
To the bus or train.
She felt unheard,
Deflated, shamed:
Had nowhere to go,
Couldn't get away:
From loneliness,
Fear, parents' fights,
Mother storming out,
Driving off, returning
Unhappy, alienated.

E. coped with the chaos
By taking control
As much as she could
Of her world:
Helping mother,
Not being a bother,
Doing all things well.
She got self-esteem
From father saying
"E. can do it all."

But marriage, three children,
Plus working full-time,
Had broken down

Her self-worth system;
Which had been
Based until then
On meeting external—
Even if internalized—
Achievement criteria,
Including perfection.

Thus she was constantly driven,
Had no time for relaxation,
Not even going to the gym,
Constantly frightened.
She'd lost her freedom
To make choices
From within.
At any trigger-time
She'd feel trapped inside
In any given situation.

She had become overly dependent
On her father's affirmation,
Which she had then
Transferred to her husband.
That dependency—
and decisions she regretted
Having made in college—
Left her doubting
Her own wisdom
And intuition.

In her marriage,
She was afraid
To disagree with
Her husband, let alone
Say what she wanted
To do or not do,
Or to challenge him

About the strict budget
He enforced, even
About buying food.

In a conjoint session,
He said he's fine with
Her asserting herself and
Saying what she wants
Or doesn't want to do—
That in fact he'd welcome
Discussions like that.

He speaks crisply
And confidently,
And I notice her
Cowering a bit,
Being almost afraid
To look at him.
But his invitation
Seemed genuine.

After that, I encouraged
Her to try it—to
Speak up to him.
After all, as she said,
She's the one who knows
The needs of the household
And the children—
Not to mention her own needs!

She had the same
Difficulty at her job
As Special Education
Supervisor—a highly
Responsible and well-
Respected position,
Which I could hear

She handled very well;
And she was told as much
Directly by the Principal.

She feared anyone
Being displeased with her,
Being critical
Like her mother.
But she and I became aware
That if she didn't speak up,
She felt trapped inside.

That insight was
Very freeing for her.

She increasingly told me
More and more
About her past—her
Childhood and youth,
Her acting out in college,
Her guilt, doubting
Her desirability or
Lovability, self-worth.

I affirmed her openness,
I warmly and attentively
Received her revelations
And affirmed especially
Her remarkably noncritical,
Loving, and patient
Support of her one
Daughter's fears, which
Reminded her of her own.

She would listen to the
Daughter's fears,
Then patiently talk

And walk the six-year-old
Through them cognitively,
While assuring the girl
That she could manage
The scary situation
And would be all right.

While telling me this,
She almost immediately
Made the connection to
What she and I were
Doing in Therapy,
And that she can do
The same for herself.

She did begin speaking up
With her husband,
And though at times
He'd grumble,
He accepted her authority,
And usually went along
With her ideas,
Wishes, suggestions.

At work, she began
To stand firm even
In the face of teachers
Being unhappy at times
With her decisions.

The more she did this—
Asserted herself, took stands,
Even gently—the more a
Solid inner core
Developed. I envisioned
An inner psychic embryo
Of her adult female
Self, growing.

That was a piece of
What I saw in her eyes.

She began to set limits
On others' demands—
Even her own inner drive
To be always busy.
She had brought up
Her ambivalence
About having time for herself:
That giving herself space
Also made her anxious,
Made room for disturbing
Feelings and memories,

But talking about them
Increasingly set her free.

She realized that Therapy
Is a place she can
Take a break from busy-ness
And rest in a love and
Affirmation of herself,
Even when doing nothing,
Just being.

She spoke no more of shame;
Even sexual energy
Could be safely conveyed,
Exchanged through the eyes.

All the above was there,
Seen, shared, asserted,
Received, and reflected back
To her through that
Meeting of our eyes
As she entered our
Sacred healing space.

ENGAGING AGING

On a winter weekend,
At the Frick Museum,
I saw Rembrandt

Looking at me
From a self-portrait
With aged eyes;

My breath caught,
I almost choked,
Deeply moved.

His shocking honesty,
Sober-faced
Self-recognition,

Probably prepared me
To honestly face
My own aging.

"Okay, this is me,"
He seemed to be saying:
"Still painting";

Defiantly
Engaging
His aging.

Aging, aged,
Yes, but
Still alive.

"That energy
Which lives in
This body-me

Will outlast me,
Remain free.
Enliven paint.

So you can see
My form frozen,
But Spirit alive:

Spirit in time:
Eternity living
In temporality."

So too
May it be
With me.

CHARCOAL HEADSTONE TRACINGS

Remember those charcoal tracings of vertical cemetery headstones that
were all the rage in the seventies. Years ago, I saw a photo of one
in   some journal illustrating an article about grieving. This trac-   ing
had a   bold dark charcoal "X" overlaying the entire tracing.   My first
thought   was "Isn't this over-kill." I mean, the headstone   itself is a
strong hint   that the subject is death, and maybe remem-   brance. But
this image res-   onated deeply, pierced my heart while   my breath said
Yes! The head-   stone marks death but at the same   time a life lived.
Why the added X?   What came to mind is some-   thing along the lines
of a double negative   making a positive: only   by dying do we come
alive; every second the   old passes away,   the new comes; my iden-
tity changes every second,   even though   there's enough continuity
that I hardly notice the death—   unless   some major or unusual event
occurs—such as this image   "X".   Years later I am loving writing
about it. Our lives are book-   ended   by physical nonexistence—
marked at the beginning   by birth and   indelibly at the end by death.
But life—Life—goes   on—not a particular   person-who-has-died's
life—but Existence   continues, such that I'm   alive with Life which
enables me to no-   tice this photo and be gripped   by its truth: the truth
that there is   Something beyond us that must be   timeless, but lives
in us tem-   porally—in time, and each person's life   pulses with Life
around   and through that "X," which reminds us that   we're dying
even   as we're also coming alive every second. Every life   is "x"-ed
out   by death every second and at the same time enlivened a-   new
until each person's life is surrendered to Life at the last death.

www.ingramcontent.com/pod-product-compliance
Lightning Source LLC
Chambersburg PA
CBHW071054090426
42737CB00013B/2348